L 25

C000243233

Through the Garden Gate

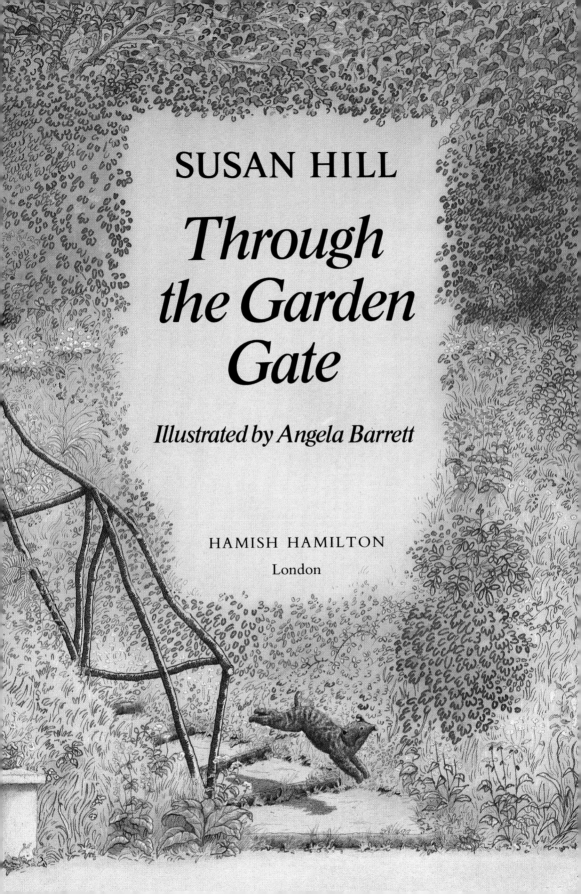

SUSAN HILL

Through the Garden Gate

Illustrated by Angela Barrett

HAMISH HAMILTON

London

First published in Great Britain 1986
by Hamish Hamilton Ltd
27 Wrights Lane London W8 5TZ

Text copyright © 1986 by Susan Hill
Illustrations copyright © 1986 by Angela Barratt

British Library Cataloguing in Publication Data

Hill, Susan, *1942-*
Through the garden gate.
1. Gardening
I. Title
635   SB450.97
ISBN 0-241-11930-8

Typeset by MS Filmsetting Ltd, Frome, Somerset
Printed and bound in Italy by
Arnoldo Mondadori Editore, Verona

The Gardens of
My Childhood

GARDENS played a large part in my life as a child, but those I remember most clearly, those which featured so vividly in my play and, most particularly, in my inner life of fantasies and dreams, were not real gardens at all, but imaginary ones. And the first and most important one of all, a garden which has haunted me for the rest of my life, so that I only have to visit it in my mind to be at once soothed, delighted and refreshed, was the garden in *Alice in Wonderland*. That remains perfect, I know every detail of it, every plant, every shrub. I could wander freely among the beds and borders, up and down the broad paths in the summer sunshine.

And yet, when I return to the book itself, to find that garden, I see that there is, in fact, very little detailed description, all is invitation and suggestion.

"She knelt down and looked along the passage into the loveliest garden you ever saw. How she longed to get out of that dark hall and wander about among those beds of bright flowers and those cool fountains."

Little enough, and yet everything one
wants from a garden is somehow there sug-
gested – the tantalising glimpse of this magical place of brightness and growth and mov-
ing water, in which one may freely stroll,
beyond the gloomy, inner room in which one
is at present trapped – a metaphor for para-
dise, indeed.

A few years later, I came upon the second
fictional garden which beckoned to me, the
one found by Mary Lennox; beyond the
overhanging swathes of ivy, the high wall and
the locked gate, lay "the secret garden", place
of sadness and silence, yet also of love and new

life, tended with such care and skill, and all in secret, haunted by birds, and by memories of past events. That garden became my refuge and my joy, a place I also could visit at will, for the key to its door is given to all who read Frances Hodgson Burnett's book.

But I had real gardens, and these, too, became places as much of the imagination as of real life. The first of them was poor and uninteresting enough, in all truth, and did not even belong to us, but to the owners of the tall, grey house in which we had an attic flat. They, a crippled old woman and her unmarried daughter, lived on the ground floor, with all their windows overlooking the front and side gardens, and the suburban crescent, beyond the privet hedge, whereas our view was only of rooftops and the sky. So I was sometimes allowed to play in that garden – provided always that I did not venture onto the flowerbeds, take any ball or wheeled toy there, pick, dig, or wear shoes which might make marks upon the lawn.

One would have thought that here was some very special place of rare plants and prize greensward, upon which hours of professional skill were lavished. Not so; it was a small, square, plain patch, at least in actuality, though in fantasy I could make anything I liked of it, and to my best recollections no one ever sowed any seed there, or tended any plant, or indeed cared much for it in any way, though once a week a bald, cross man mowed the grass and weeded between the rose bushes.

Yet I spent many happy hours there, and places which figure so largely in the everyday lives of small children assume an importance and a charm which bears little relation to reality. Such flowers and bushes as there were I knew in microscopic detail and at every season, and they also figured as characters with whom I conversed. It made me feel even closer to Alice, when she went through the looking glass into that other garden, the one of live flowers.

I do not know who ever could originally have planned and planted that garden in which I played, but it cannot have been anyone with an eye for beauty or suitability, for there were more over-large, unattractive or just plain dull things than can often have been assembled within such a small space – great dark, dank laurel and mahonia bushes, huge hydrangeas, conifers, a tall privet hedge, too much cotoneaster, and a laburnum, of whose yellow, pendant flowers and twisted little pods I was taught to go in dread, because just one of them could kill me stone dead on the spot if it so much as brushed against my lips. So that, ever since, I have seen pure evil not as something dark but as something beckoningly bright, fascinatingly, deceitfully, abundantly yellow.

But there were a few things of prettiness or delight – rows of London Pride, all among the rockery which bordered the path, some huge old flag irises, velvet pansies, aconites under a beech in February; and a great philadelphus whose creamy petals and heavy scent transfixed me. Now, I only have to catch a breath of it to be catapulted back, to stand under that spreading bush, drunk and drowsy on the smell.

Away from home, there was another world of gardens, for we lived in a town whose public pride was set forth in them, and every day, in all weathers, we walked among them. If I close my eyes, I can still go straight to each one, down its every path, around the corners, making my way without faltering; through the Italian gardens, with flat pools and stone statues, flights of steps and grottoes; down the winding cliff paths which led to the sea shore, in whose steep gardens, sheltered by trees, thousands of snowdrops, primroses, celandines and violets flowered in spring; into the scented gardens for the blind, and the rose gardens, and the miniature garden, where a tiny waterfall cascaded over rocks to a little lake, and an island was reached over a small, hump-backed bridge, which had a wooden boathouse, and a boat, the Blue Boy, moored beside it, forever waiting for its phantom rower. Even at the age of four or less, I was conscious of the hugeness of my own limbs when I stood before it all, felt myself to be already a giant, my feet too big to walk the gravel paths, able, if I were admitted into it, to bestride that little kingdom like a Gulliver. It was there, I think, that I first understood regret for a lost past (even though, in this case, it was a past that never was), and the bitter frustration of Alice, when she grew too large to get through the tiny door that led into the beautiful garden.

Potted Gardens

THERE are very few places out of which some kind of garden cannot be made. Even in the gloomiest square of back yard, dark and dank below towering city houses; in a side passageway; or a rough area of concrete or bald paving slabs; on a window ledge; in a porch; on a flat roof or the tiniest balcony; outside the front door of an apartment – on, or in or around, above or beside any of these, you may gain great pleasure simply by planting your garden in pots. And even if you have far more space to boast of, wide terraces, a vast lawn, a broad driveway, flowers in tubs and containers will always enhance the scene still more.

A great many more things than you might imagine will thrive in pots. Try anything, provided its roots do not want to probe down too deep or stretch too far along, or it should not naturally grow very tall.

In the spring, it is the easiest thing to choose from the boxes of bedding plants on sale at every corner shop. The varieties are common enough but none the worse for that, if chosen with care, and a lot of one colour and one kind, all put together, look better than a little bit of this and a little bit of that, anxiously mingled. Dozens of all-white petunias, or

sugar-pink snapdragons or the darkest purple pansies, clots of Cambridge blue lobelia, some trailing, others not, and a copper pan filled with French marigolds. Put your plants in anything you have to hand, the more containers the merrier. Put them in flower pots, old and new, large and small, straight-sided or fat-bellied, in grand terracotta pots with edges crimped like pastry, or stone urns with swagged handles; in wooden tubs, round and square, weather-stained or white-painted; in wicker baskets, lined with moss; old baths, basins, buckets and chamber pots, wheelbarrows, kettles, jugs and sinks and troughs. And for your indoor garden, search on second-hand stalls and in jumble sales for old glass dishes and china bowls, cracked cups and mugs and jugs, in which to plant bulbs that will see you through the dark days of winter.

Humble flowers look happy in pots, but things more rarefied and exquisite such as camellias will also do well, and lilies thrive

best grown in tubs, when the soil can be exactly prepared to suit their fussy, individual natures, and they may be moved about, according to requirements of sun and shade and shelter. Put roses in tubs, and lavender and bay and fuchsias, though dreary little stunted conifers, all of the same dull green, are a waste of any good container. Herbs grow well when confined within bounds, for too many have a spreading and straggling and invasive habit. Pots of parsley and mint and thyme, basil and tarragon, rosemary and marjoram and chervil, can line the kitchen window ledge, or be set out in a row beside the back door, for easy picking.

Some of the tastiest tomatoes are grown in flowerpots out of doors, even in a poor aspect and cloudy summer, if they are well and religiously fed and watered, and firmly staked. Sweetest of all are the tiny Gardener's Delights.

A French bean, started by an eager child in

a jam jar, will transfer to a very large pot and within a month or two give enough pods for a generous meal, and in a wide-based container, one courgette plant grown up from seed will flower, all golden and gaudy, and then fruit gladly.

Put a pip or a stone in a small pot, one from lemon or orange, grape or avocado, peach or apricot, apple, pear, plum and nurture the shoot carefully, sheltering it indoors through autumn and winter and early spring. In summer, set it out in the sunshine, pot it on with restraint each year, and you may end with a glorious tree, though perhaps it will never fruit. And a veritable orchard can be established in the smallest area of garden using only trees grown in tubs, if the right dwarfing stock is selected.

If you have a balcony or a bit of fence or trellis, post or rail or line, a clematis, a climbing rose and all manner of sweet peas will root in a tub and soon clamber up and run along and spread out to cover the ugliness beneath.

The Kitchen Garden

"WITH the best will in the world, it's difficult to pretend that the parsnip is really
eatable but it's an immense and exacting
pleasure to grow. At the start of the season
you grub out a row of pits with a trowel and
fill them almost to the brim with finely
sieved soil. Then you poke into each soft dell
about a dozen of the crisp wafers which are
the parsnip seeds and pat earth over them.
Come the summer, you pull out all but one of
the seedlings from each cluster – pale gold
pencils with feathery tops, which it always
gives you a pang to throw onto the compost
heap, though there's nothing else to be done
with them. Then, as the winter approaches,
the great spreading leaves of the survivors rot
and yellow and the parsnips withdraw into
their subterranean existence until, some time
after Christmas, the time comes to crack the
frosty crust over them and lug them out,
gross, whiskered and reeking, from their
lairs."

John Carey

"As vegetable gardeners aren't primarily concerned with eating, they harbour, like librarians, a tidy-minded dislike of anyone who actually wants to use the commodities they're in charge of. To have to uproot cabbages, say, from a row, and hand them over for cooking, is always an annoyance. The gaps look unsightly, like snapped-off teeth. A stalwart, unbroken line of cabbages, on the other hand, with their hearts tight as fists and their purple outer leaves spread to catch the dew, raises your spirits every time you visit them."

John Carey

"We have our first dish of peas. The aisles of bean plants grow tall and the green walls are full of bulging pods. Annie says she will pick the peas for dinner, but we rush to the garden to do it ourselves, excited at the start of yet another harvest. Compared with the gathering of strawberries, pea-picking is intricate but undramatic. There is no sudden glow of crimson, no soft warmth of fruit. It is a world of shapes, pea being distinguishable from leaf only by reason of its bulk and form. We pick by feeling rather than by sight. The pea plant is a gentle green, deep and soft against the pale colour of the lettuces that shelter from the sun in the shade of the pea rows. Our baskets are full of hard, rattling pods, we pull lettuces for salad. It is good to feed oneself from one's own earth."

Clare Leighton

"When I am free to take a quiet stroll for pure pleasure of the garden, I take it among the vegetables."

Gertrude Jekyll

A friend of mine was visiting a great country house which has a famous garden, but because it was a Bank Holiday and the main areas were becoming crowded, he walked away from the roses and the fountains, the theatre lawn and the pleached walk, in the direction of a long high wall, beyond which, he knew, lay the kitchen gardens. There, at the wrought-iron gate leading into them, he met the Lady of the House, who told him politely that he had mistaken his way, and was strolling in an area not open to the public. "For,"

said she, "beyond here are only the vegetables, and *whoever would want to look at those?*"

Yet a well-tended kitchen garden is a joy to behold at almost any season, and a pleasure to work in, too, not only productive and useful, but ordered, decorative, even elegant. The satisfaction of seeing one's own food growing is a perpetual one and never to be despised, and the joy of picking, and. pulling up, the first early potatoes, squeaky pea pods, earthy little carrots, lettuces green as grass, is a fine one.

Almost anyone with a bit of ground can have a successful kitchen garden. The area does not have to be particularly large. Indeed, plenty of vegetables can be grown in tubs and other containers, or gro-bags on balconies, and up canes and trellises in porches.

The soil needs to be lovingly prepared, stone-free, well-dug and sifted, well-manured, and in as sunny a spot as possible, not too far away from both the kitchen itself and a handy tool-shed. You can learn as you go along, from books and magazines and newspapers, seed catalogues and packets, other gardeners, by trial and error. There is no mystique. Use good, stout tools, take your time, be prepared for failure, be flexible in your whole approach to the growing of vegetables.

The larger the plot, the greater the amount of work required, but the demands of a kitchen garden can be kept in check. The first essential is to plan ahead, and the first rule and most useful thing to remember is that you do not *have* to grow any vegetable you do not care for. A big kitchen garden with neat rows crammed with every conceivable variety is best in the hands of professionals, or at least those of long experience, with a great deal of time and energy and assistance. It is an ideal, but it is a bad mistake to take a small plot and try to grow a few of everything in it. No one tries to grow every flower that exists in their own garden, but it is surprising how many people slave over onions and carrots, parsnips and potatoes, turnips and swede, marrows and cucumber, peas and beans, radishes and rhubarb, beetroot and artichokes, sprouts, cabbage, cauliflower, broccoli, lettuces, tomatoes, and all manner of herbs.

First, make a list of every vegetable you can think of, common or rare, root, leaf and pod. Consult gardening manuals; canvas family and friends. Now, carefully prune this list of every vegetable you do not like, or would only rarely want to eat.

Next, consider how many very common vegetables are left which you can buy of good quality, readily and cheaply from any shop. There is little point in using up precious space on maincrop potatoes, carrots or swede. What can be bought is generally good and inexpensive. If your only reason for growing vegetables is to save money, you must cost out meticulously your seed, plants, tools, fertiliser and manure, pesticide and time, and then make an allowance for crop failure from disease, pests, poor seed, bad weather, rotting in store. You may well find that your crop is an uneconomic one, and the difference between a home-grown, large onion, and a shop-bought one is very slight.

Next, consider your own site, soil and weather conditions. A very light, sandy loam will give you wonderful young carrots, a thick, heavy clay will not. If you have nearby trees harbouring pigeons, brassicas will have to be well-netted; if you are plagued by mice and smaller birds, great efforts will be necessary to protect peas and beans from the moment they are sown.

Now, select all vegetables which you greatly enjoy and eat in quantity, particularly if they are expensive or difficult to buy and if their flavour when home-grown and freshly picked is incomparably better than any in the market. You may settle finally on a dozen varieties, only three or four, or perhaps even just one, so that you aim to become a specialist new potato, pea, bean or salad crop grower. If you put all your eggs into one basket in this way, you will also put all your energy, time, care, love and growing expertise there too, and may have prize crops, admired and envied for miles around. A whole garden full of peas and beans of every possible kind, to be sown from November until July, eaten from May until Christmas, would be an object of pride, delight and envy. You would have the finest crop, to eat fresh, sell, freeze or dry. You would have first peas, mid-season peas and late peas, mange-touts, sugar-snap peas, and petit pois, broad beans, runner beans and French beans, white, purple, and darkest green, and a kitchen garden full of flowers, too, attracting bees and butterflies. There is a great deal to be said for being a specialist in the kitchen garden.

Special favourites

Mange-tout

Erect a frame with stakes or tall canes, sinking them deep into the soil, strong enough to withstand the wind and the weight of the plants when full-grown. Some varieties will climb to eight feet. Weed the plants and pick the crop regularly, to encourage further growth.

Purple and white sprouting broccoli

The shoots are tender as asparagus, quickly steamed, covered in melted butter. Broccoli fills a hunger-gap in March, when there are few fresh vegetables about. It is prolific and nourishing, and little trouble, though susceptible to hard winters and a few pests. Sow in March, plant out in July.

Celeriac

Sow in April, plant shallowly in July, water very copiously to swell the roots. Delicious, peculiar flavour, very versatile, full of iron. Expensive to buy in the market.

Chard

The easiest of all vegetables to grow, and the most useful, being two-for-the-price-of-one, a leafy vegetable, like spinach, with the stalk, to be steamed, or boiled, and eaten like cooked celery, or use raw in salads. Crops all summer and autumn, encouraged by regular picking, dies right down in winter, and rises up again like magic in spring for a second cropping, before finally running to seed. If I had only one vegetable, it would be chard.

Courgettes

Sow two seeds to a small peat pot in March, and set out on a sunny window-ledge. Plant out in late May or early June when all frosts are over. Feed and water well, cut regularly. Prolific, decorative, delicious. Become marrows if left.

Pleasures of the kitchen garden

WHITE flowers on early peas and beans.

Scarlet flowers, climbing up wigwams and tents of runner beans in high summer.

Gaudy orange flowers opening in the early morning sun on courgettes and marrows.

Leeks in orderly rows, their tops falling up-and-over like guardsmen's bearskins.

Beads of dew resting on the crinkled inner leaves of cabbages, like crystal drops.

The earthiness of new potatoes, just dug up.

The sweetness of stolen peas, eaten raw.

Leaning on the spade.

Frozen fingers tingling back to life around a mug of hot soup, after winter digging.

The first thin green line of seedlings down the dark soil.

Baskets piled high with a glut of anything.

Plaiting onions into strings in the garden shed, with rain pattering on the roof above.

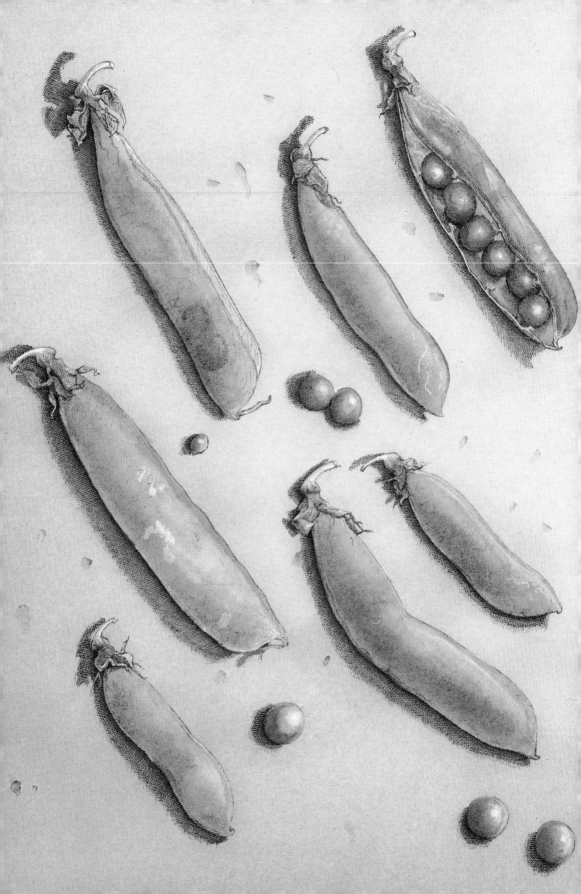

The Herb Garden

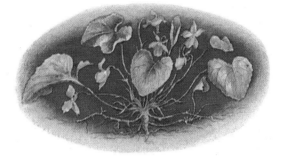

NEAR to the house, have a few herbs. They are not all decorative, many will spread wildly unless you keep them hard in check, others look straggly, like hair left uncut. Be firm with thyme, ruthless with sage and mint. Best of all, confine the spreaders in pots.

Unless you are besotted with herbs, an exotic and experimental cook, want to emulate the Elizabethans with their herb gardens, or concoct strange medicinal potions, beware herb plants which have names you have only read of in dim and dusty volumes of ancient receipts. They will clutter up your herb patch and be of neither use nor ornament, particularly once the lettering on the labels has been weathered away.

A little rosemary goes a long way. It is very pungent, and though it looks tough, is surprisingly vulnerable in hard winters.

You can never have too much parsley. It is temperamental, slow to germinate, may dislike your garden and refuse to thrive at all, but once it takes, you will be well rewarded. Sow it thickly, in long rows. It is said to do well in households where the wife wears the trousers.

Basil is wonderful married to tomatoes. It easily straggles and runs to seed, does not like the cold or wet, and as often as not will up and die when transplanted. Sow in pots and keep it in the kitchen on a sunny window-ledge, well watered but never waterlogged. Pinch off the flower tops regularly. Pull a leaf and rub it between your fingers, or even just brush against the plant and a marvellous, musky smell is released.

Tarragon is tougher than it appears. It will often survive severe frosts and cold when all about it other plants succumb. Best with eggs and chicken, but ensure that your tarragon is French, not the bushier, smaller-leaved Russian variety, which is bitter and inedible.

Fennel with fish and for feathery foliage.

Chervil. "The leaf that rejoices the heart." Exceptionally pretty, lacey and delicate, a subtle, mild flavour, good with eggs or in mayonnaise and summer soups.

Thyme for treading underfoot, attracting bees, luxuriant flowers, for eating with game and treating sore throats.

Municipal Gardens

O THE joy of the municipal park, that most urban of all gardens, with rules that apply nowhere else and a character all of its own.

O the joy of the bandstand, planted all around with deckchairs on a summer afternoon, and ice-cream sellers and Ooom-Pah Ooom-Pah, Souza and *South Pacific*.

And the duck pond with mallards gravely swimming among the toy sailing boats, veering easily away from the children's poles, gorged on bread. And the broad gravelled walks and the statue of Queen Victoria, the rustic wooden shelter and the benches dedicated to dead dignitaries and long-serving groundsmen, the referee's whistle and the sad old ladies and the man with his broom and metal cart for litter and leaves, and the happy, happy swings.

Go through the garden gate of the municipal park and you are in a land where rules of bedding out and floral display and pruning and clipping are applied as rigidly and unchangingly as the printed list of bye-laws importantly displayed. Here the seasons are ordained precisely by the calendar, year after year. On this date, the pansies are set out and on that petunias today, the wallflowers are always lifted. On this day, goal posts are erected or dismantled and if it is summer, there the man on the mower will be, riding up and down, up and down, in the straightest of lines.

What you would never dream of doing in any private garden, here the park gardeners do to perfection. Flower beds in the shape of lozenges or kidneys or half moons are carved as with razor blades out of the turf, and within them, where no weed may raise its head, all is arranged strictly according to height, with the tallest plants at the back tied tight to their stakes, and low on the ground at the front, alyssum or bachelor buttons, mesambryanthemums and tight little French marigolds.

Here, scarlet and blood-red, acid yellow and sunburst orange are carefully, artistically matched.

In spring, thousands of waxen tulips stand,

unable to bend or stir, and on the first day of June the dahlias spring fully grown from their hothouse. Here is a scented rose-garden for the blind, there a meticulous rockery, where purple ericas hold sway, and between the flower beds, clumps of dark and gloomy shrubs, rhododendrons, mahonia, laurestinus, grown elephantine, with secret hollows beneath into which the children may creep and hide.

And O the joy of the floral clock, so accurate, in bronze and white, planned out as on graph paper down to the last half second, but all growing, all alive.

And in winter, when the boughs of the park trees are bare black against the pinking sky at frosty tea-time, there is the viburnum, with its pink blossom to soften the flowerless-ness and sweeten the cold.

In these gardens there are real gardeners, with spades and barrows and little huts set behind a beech hedge, men with muddy boots and patient faces, and always, some-where, the scritch-scratch of a hoe.

Here, all is order and geometry, mess and muddle are banished, growth kept within bounds.

All is predictable and safe.

This is a place of very particular and civilized gardeners' pleasure.

Into the Rose Garden

NO FLOWER is better known or more commonly found than the rose, none has such a romantic place in literature, symbol of love and youthful sweetness, beauty and death. No garden is complete without one, no plant is more obliging, versatile, various, full of charm, none can be so delightful or so dull, so easy and yet so temperamental. A bald bed full of nothing but modern roses can be the ugliest sight in the garden, a hideous mix of crude colours, scarlet as a temptress's nails, acid yellow and loud pink, or else unnaturally variegated. The shape of such bushes is leggy,

spindly and ragged, all bare below, or else the plants have been tormented and tortured, clipped and forced, into a terrible neatness.

They will flower anywhere, neglected, ill-treated, or they will succumb to blot and blotch, spot and mould, and aphid, be intolerant of too rich a soil or too poor, too little rain or too much. They may have blooms of surpassing beauty, vicious thorns and unsightly suckers.

Yet roses are the most seductive and breath-takingly beautiful of all flowers, creamy or silvery white, shell or blush or faded pink, deepest blood and purple-red, lemon and sunshine and moonlight yellow, tight or flat open, inward or outward curving, frilled or plain, grey or budded or pale green or bronze or dark of foliage, upright, spreading, bushy habit, thick-set or delicate, gaudy or subtle, blowsy or modest.

A rose will clamber and ramble obligingly over tree or trellis or arbour or arch, door mantel, wall, post or fence.

Plant some of the most fragrant beneath your window and sit beside it, or train one up the wall and right along the bedroom sill, then lie in bed on a June night and sleep a heady sleep, drugged by the scent.

Choose your roses and mingle them carefully, some old, some new, some common, others rare and hard to find, some to grow into great shrubs, others to fringe a low wall, some to ramble, others to be neatly bedded out and a few in tubs close to the house, and you will then have flowers from early June until a mild Christmas Day.

When roses are not rambling wildly, almost out of sight, they are best as old-fashioned shrubs in a border. They are sturdy and robust and long-lived, they are little trouble, and often have the richest of scents, especially if they are damask roses, and the largest, showiest, or the smallest, most exquisite of blossoms.

Prepare their bed with care, for they are going to live here long. Choose a site that drains well. Dig two spits deep, then pile rich old compost and manure into the trench. Set the shrubs well apart, to give them air and space and light and room for good growth. All they will require thereafter is a little pruning back of dead wood, once they are well established, and a comforting mulch of old leaves and straw.

Rose Ladies

Dame Prudence	Wife of Bath
Francesca	Felicia
Penelope	Jenny Wren
Lady Curzon	Lady Hillingdon
Duchesse d'Angouleme	Duchesse de Verneuil
Empress Josephine	Queen of Denmark
Madame Plantier	Madame Hardy
Louise Odier	Aimee Vibert
Bourbon Queen	La Reine Victoria
Cecile Brunner	Claire Jacquier
Ena Harkness	Kathleen Harrop
Madame Alfred	Madame Caroline
Carriere	Testout
Mrs Herbert Stevens	Mrs Sam McGredy
Albertine	Evangeline
Amy Robsart	Meg Merilees
Lady Sylvia	Lady Belper
Lili Marlene	Violet Carson
Queen Elizabeth	Dainty Bess

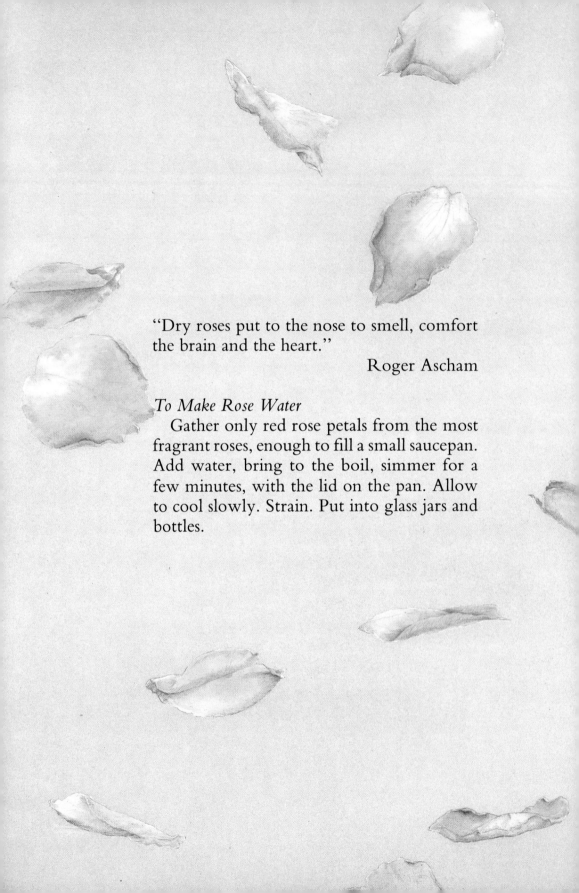

"Dry roses put to the nose to smell, comfort the brain and the heart."

Roger Ascham

To Make Rose Water
   Gather only red rose petals from the most fragrant roses, enough to fill a small saucepan. Add water, bring to the boil, simmer for a few minutes, with the lid on the pan. Allow to cool slowly. Strain. Put into glass jars and bottles.

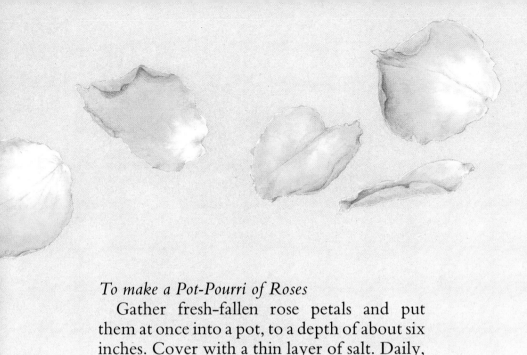

To make a Pot-Pourri of Roses

Gather fresh-fallen rose petals and put them at once into a pot, to a depth of about six inches. Cover with a thin layer of salt. Daily, or weekly, add more rose petals, as well as those of one or two other heavily scented flowers – pinks, philadelphus, sweet geranium. Cover each layer again with salt, and close the jar tightly each time. When the jar is almost full add a quarter of an ounce of cloves, and some dried orange peel. Open the jar to allow the scent to fill the room. Close again tightly.

Ten Delights
of a Garden

WHITE flowers.

An archway cut into a tall hedge.

A circular seat built about the trunk of a tree.

Small birds bathing in a stone trough.

Wooden wheelbarrows, set with geraniums.

Rhubarb plants left to spread and tower and run all to seed.

Sunflowers in rows in early September.

The smell of tomato plants inside a conservatory.

Pincushion moss growing in the crevices of a stone wall.

A stretch of freshly turned earth, fingered over by frost.

Children's Gardens

"THERE's the old azalea garden behind. They say that this place must have been made for children."   Rudyard Kipling

For children, gardens are magical places. A small garden will quite suffice, a large one will seem huge, and the landscaped parkland of some great country house is another country.

There will always be places to hide and seek; behind tall hedges, or down low to the ground under small ones; underneath wide-spreading bushes and shrubs, or in the very centre of them; pressed up close to the wall behind swags of hanging wisteria and winter-flowering jasmine; inside arbours, summer-houses, grottos, potting sheds, toolsheds, greenhouses or conservatories; beneath trees and among trees, at the back of trees and inside the boles of trees; around the fruit canes, the bean poles, the pea frames or the currant bushes.

There are places to run; down pleached walks and grassy alleys, up crazy paving and stone-flagged and sunken brick paths, and across lawns and along gravelled terraces. There are trees and fences and walls to climb, grassy banks down which to roll, branches from which to swing; plant pots may be piled up and barrows wheeled, earth and water stirred into mud, bonfires built, sticks and stakes cut for lances and swords and tent poles. Noise may be made freely, apples and plums and cherries and sweet new carrots and peas purloined.

And to be a child quite alone in a garden is a wonder and a mystery, for then there is time and space and silence, in which to watch things stir and shift, rustle and scuttle. There is picking to do, and a thousand tiny creatures to be close-watched, tracked, touched. It is very fine to sit in the strong branch of a tree and look up into the clouds and then down to the ground, thinking, swaying, observing but unobserved, to swing peacefully to and fro, to and fro, creak-creak, to smell the outdoor smells, to reflect, to dream, to plot.

But whether children will garden in a garden is quite another matter. If they will not, there is no forcing them, for then gardening will become just another task instigated by adults, to be got through anyhow, with no

point or pleasure in any of it. Who would want to instil into their children a lifetime's loathing of gardens and all to do with and in them? But suggestion and encouragement may work wonders and if the response is even a little enthusiastic, seize the moment.

Before you give them a garden, know that you must be prepared to do at the least half, and in all likelihood rather more, of the work. They will not, or cannot, do much of serious digging, weeding, hoeing, raking, staking, pruning, clipping. They will plant and sow, dig holes, puddle in, water, pull, pick and poke about, and tramp up and down in wellington boots, firming the earth. But if it is too cold or too wet, too hot or too dry, they will not do anything.

Choose for them one of the best spots in the whole of your garden, with good sun and a little shelter, south or west facing, and with excellent soil. Do not insult them with a neglected, weed-ridden, stone-filled patch, against a wall or a deeply-rooted tree or an ivy-covered fence. If you do not want to be bothered with such a corner, why should they? If nothing will grow for the most experienced and ingenious and hard-working

of adult gardeners, why should it grow for them?

There must be a fertile soil, well dug, manured, evened and raked by you, and made all ready for planting and sowing at just the right time. Then things will shoot up, flower, flourish and spread.

Their garden must be easily accessible and prominent, so that things may readily be shown off to visitors, and large enough to be a real and proper garden, not a baby thing, but not so large as to dishearten and prove unmanageable.

A great deal may very satisfactorily be packed into a compact area and give the interest of wide variety.

"Bulbs are the beginner's best friends."

Bury them like treasure at the tail end of the year, to be found with unexpected joy in early spring.

Shopping for bulbs, picking out the tight, wizened, queerly shaped little corms from full boxes, or choosing from the glowing pictures in an Aladdin's cave of a catalogue is one of the best pleasures of gardening, and a lot of money need not be spent. Be generous with snowdrops, single and double, and crocuses, butter coloured and vivid orange, deep purple or pure white, with pink and white and blue anemone blanda which will come up like stars, tulips small and tall, palest blue chionodoxa, delicate, sweet-scented iris reticulata, waving daffodils and narcissi to put heart into the grey March mornings.

And there are bulbs for producing summer flowers, gladioli, tall irises, even lilies, which may all be grown with pride by children.

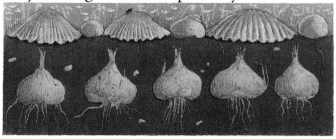

Much joy comes from scattering seeds up and down and all about. Prettily dressed-up boxes, expensively produced "For Children", may safely be resisted, and far less money spent on better-chosen packets of flowers. Love-in-a-mist, clarkia, night-scented stocks, cornflowers, marigolds, virginia creeper, will come up very readily, if well watered after sowing.

In the children's garden, there should be some quick growing things and others requiring more patience, though always remembering that a small matter of four weeks is a weary wait to the young. Therefore, instant gardens are never to be despised, so that the pleasure in seeing something established and vigorous in their plot will help them through the time it takes for seeds to sprout. Bought bedding-out plants and a few small flowering shrubs will transform the bare ground into a garden.

Also have:

A wigwam of canes up which runner beans or sweet peas can climb.

Vegetables. Radishes grow faster than anything else at all. They may be pulled, washed, and tied into bunches to be given away as gifts, for the children will not eat them.

Things that spread and run and become enormous. Courgettes and marrows and pumpkins may all be begun in small peat pots on the window-ledge, one fat seed to a pot, and set out in later May when the frosts are past. They will flower gaudily in the early morning summer sun and give good fruits. But the children will not eat them. They are for watching and measuring, picking and weighing, carving out or presenting to teachers.

Runner beans and French beans. Also best begun on window-ledges from just one bean, grown on blotting paper in a jam jar; a mighty structure which has to be supported

and staked will cheerfully grow.

Potatoes. These should be bought in January, and set out on the windowsill in trays, the green sprouts, all but two or three, to be rubbed off daily. And the potatoes planted in the ground on Good Friday, in the way of all good old country gardeners. In June, they can be pulled, when the size of birds' eggs. These the children *may* eat.

Children have small and clumsy fingers. They cannot transplant fragile seedlings or sow the finest seed thinly. They should be given sturdy plants and fat seeds and small, strong tools. But grass seed can be very thickly sown, to come up quickly as a patch of vivid green lawn.

There can easily be an apple or pear tree of the dwarf variety, though the wait for fruit will be an exercise in patience.

The importance of correct and frequent watering will be quickly learnt, and particularly so, the art of the hose.

If there are well-loved pets, there should be a well-fenced garden plot, or else much anger and distress will ensue. All small, mobile mammals will eat the produce, and dogs and cats will dig and trample.

The eternal conflict that rages in the breast of every good gardener between a love for his garden and a love of wild creatures, will be very early experienced when the activities of

birds, mice, slugs, rabbits or squirrels are witnessed.

But once any of the pleasure, excitement, satisfaction and solace to be derived from gardening has been enjoyed, the memory of it will never dim. He who is a happy gardener as a small child, is a happy gardener for life.

In Praise of the Wilderness

THE best gardens are something of a muddle. They have an air of happy accident, they look a little careless, however carefully in fact the whole has been planned. Things have grown up and flourished cheek by jowl, like a large family of children, some natural, some adopted, some short and some tall, some further advanced for their age than others, some with red hair, others golden, some blue-eyed, others dark, and they tumble about together then fall into each other's arms, or else squabble perpetually until they are separated, in just such a way.

There is something to be said for taking chances in the garden; accept a cutting, order from a catalogue, find an old packet of seeds, and simply put things in side by side and see what will happen, rather than trying to organise every colour, every shape, every relative height in some perfect picture which will, in reality, never be perfect – this or that will fail to thrive, grow a foot too tall, be bushy rather than compact, bright blue instead of pale. Imagination may help, and observation of other gardeners' successes, and sound advice. But experiment and experience and the happy accidents of nature will make the best of gardens, and give most unexpected pleasures. And you will have all the glory of the garden for yourself, not owe it to others.

Find room for a patch of wilderness, however small, out of reach, or where the ground is too flinty or boggy or sour to cultivate, but where nettles will always grow, and rocket and campion, docks and thistles, fat hen and chickweed and seeded wild poppies and golden rod, as they grew on the bomb sites of London.

If the wilderness is up against a fence or a wall, bryony and traveller's joy and perhaps wild roses will soon come clambering up, though ruthlessness against all kinds of ivy and the pretty but deadly columbine will be essential.

Then, this tamed wilderness will be a safe haven for many butterflies and birds and all manner of insects, and the garden will be a live thing, not a dead.

"She had been in that garden before, but never in May, with the apple-blossom out and the wallflowers filling the air with their fragrance.

"Narrow paths between high, built-up banks supporting flower borders, crowded with jonquils, auriculas, forget-me-nots and other spring flowers, led from one part of the garden to another. One winding path led to the earth closet in its bower of nut-trees halfway down the garden, another to the vegetable garden and on to the rough grass plot before the beehives. Between each section were thick groves of bushes with ferns and capers and Solomon's seal, so closed in that the long, rough grass there was always damp. Wasted ground, a good gardener might have said, but delightful in its cool, green shadiness.

"Nearer the house was a portion given up entirely to flowers, not growing in beds but crammed together in an irregular square where they bloomed in half-wild profusion ... the flowers grew just as they would, in crowded masses, perfect in their imperfection."

Flora Thompson

"Our terracestrip of garden was Mother's monument, and she worked it headstrong, without plan. She would never control or clear this ground, merely cherish whatever was there. And she was as impartial in her encouragement to all that grew as a spell of sweet sunny weather. She would force nothing, graft nothing, nor set things in rows; she welcomed self-seeders, let each have its head, and was the enemy of very few weeds. Consequently our garden was a sprouting jungle and never an inch was wasted. Syringa shot up, laburnum hung down, white roses smothered the apple tree, red flowering currants (smelling sharply of foxes) spread entirely along one path; such a chaos of blossom as amazed the bees and bewildered the birds in the air. Potatoes and cabbages were planted at random among foxgloves, pansies and pinks. Often some species would entirely capture the garden – forget-me-nots one year, hollyhocks the next, then a sheet of harvest poppies. Whatever it was, one let it grow."

Laurie Lee

Plants for Butterflies

Alyssum	Aubretia
Bird's Foot Trefoil	Blackthorn
Buddleia	Bugloss
Catmint	Candytuft
Cornflower	Coltsfoot
Dog-rose	Columbine
Flag Iris	Dame's Violet
Golden Rod	Forget-me-not
Heliotrope	Hawthorn
Honesty	Honeysuckle
Ice Plant	Hyssop
Lavender	Jasmine
Lilac	Lady's Smock
Lupin	Marjoram
Mignonette	Melissa
Pinks	Petunia
Purple Loosestrife	Polyanthus
Sea thrift	Ragged Robin
Stinging nettle	Scabious
Sweet Violet	Thyme
Verbena	Wolf's Bane

The Night Garden

"My delight and thy delight,
Walking, like two angels white,
In the garden of the night."
Robert Bridges

IT IS very late. It is past midnight. Inside the house, there are still bright lights, there are chattering voices and laughter, and footsteps up and down the stairs. The children are restless, crying, padding about, for it has been a blazing July day, and even with the windows flung open wide, the heat is still in the house, the air close. Bedclothes are pushed back. No one can sleep yet. For a week the sun has shone, the ground and the air are choked with dust. Yet it is good, everyone feels younger, freer, happier in the sun – except the animals, who creep close up to the shadow of walls and bushes and pant in the heat of mid-day. But it is tiring, too, simply *being* is tiring in such a summer.

So, leave the house, the lights and the fever. Go outside, alone. Close the door behind you. Wait, for a few seconds. Breathe in deeply. Recover your balance.

Then walk, quietly, quietly, down the path, and through the garden gate.

Here in the garden, it is quite different. At last, it is cool, though during the day there was scarcely a shady place, even under the trees or behind the tall hedge, the sun found out every dark, secret corner and probed its way in, baking, drying.

But now, the sun has gone. It is dark, but not too dark, for there is a good, round moon, whitening the flowers, making the roses and the tall delphiniums, the phlox and the lupins, like pale ghostly wands, and silvering the wisteria that tumbles over the balcony.

When you leave the path, take off your

shoes and carry them. The grass is perfectly cool, just damp with the first, night dew. Walk a little further and you brush against the thyme that edges the lawn. Stop. Bend down and touch it. Smell. It is pungent, slightly smoky. And the next cluster of thyme smells more lemony than lemons themselves, and the next, spicy as cinnamon.

In the night garden in summer, the scents of the plants are always wonderful, yet who ever knows, who comes out here so late

to savour them? Sweet tobacco plants and night-scented stocks, little frilled pinks, many herbs and, up the fence, great swags of honeysuckle to take your breath away. The daytime heat destroys them all, but in the night garden, the scents make you giddy. Pick a sprig from the spiky lavender bush and crush it between your fingers. You can rub the oil into a warm crease of your neck and it will linger there to please and sweeten you till morning.

Walk on a little further, between the bushes, beside the privet hedge. There is the faintest of movement on the night air, the shadow of a breeze, just enough to shift the leaves of the great copper beech in the middle of the lawn. If you go and sit down beneath it, sit down or even lie on your back, and look up you see nothing but dense, dark, leaves. But, as they shift softly, prickles of stars and slanting moonlight. Then, still again. Dark. No air.

Somewhere beneath the hedge, a tiny creature. Scuttles. Scuttles again. Silence.

Stay here longer, and the cat will find you, padding across the grass and sliding and weaving about your person, before disappearing again, to hunt the tiny creature, evil-eyed.

Today, they mowed the grass. Go towards the compost heaps behind the shed and find the soft pile of cuttings by its smell, fresh and moist and slightly earthy, like no other smell.

Here, in the garden at night, it is another world, strange and yet friendly and familiar, never frightening. There is such quietness, such sweetness, such refreshment.

Close your eyes. Breathe in again, smell everything mingled together, flowers and earth and leaves and grass. Smell the night.

Listen. Nothing at all. Silence, rushing like the sea in your ears.

However small and sparse the garden, and wherever it is, even inside a great city, if something grows there, it is a magic place by night.

Leave it, quietly walk back towards the lights that shine out of the house. You will take its magic with you.

Now, you will sleep.

"'Twas midnight – through the lattice,
                                   wreath'd
With woodbine, many a perfume breath'd
From plants that wake when others sleep,
From timid jasmine buds, that keep
Their odour to themselves all day,
But, when the sunlight dies away
Let the delicious secret out
To every breeze that roams about."

Thomas Moore

The Winter Garden

IT IS a day in deepest January. It is the time of year when you feel like drawing the curtains tight and turning your back on the garden. Earth lies hard as iron, flowerbeds empty, branches bare.

If you read about mid-winter gardening, you are told that this is the time, indeed, the only time, when you may safely take a holiday; or else that there is plenty of work to do in a well-heated greenhouse; or that you should be sitting in an armchair, doing your garden planning, making charts and rotation plans, ordering this and that from catalogues.

Or you may have an optimistic book, one that flies in the face of what you know of nature, which extols the delights of a thousand plants that will flower abundantly from November until March, so that your winter garden need never lack bloom or beauty, if you will only apply yourself con- scientiously to organising things better.

When you glance out at your own vacant plot, it will now appear even more dejected, dull and depressing than before, because you believe that you are to blame. But read between the lines of these happy counsellors, and you will discover that they are not like you and me; that their gardens are situated in Cornwall, the Scilly Isles, face both south and west, are sheltered by high walls and long windbreaks of evergreen, so that they are never exposed to bitter winds and blackened by hard frosts; that the gardeners themselves are rich, either in money, so that they can afford to buy a dozen exotic plants and lose eleven of them to poor weather, or in time, so that they have hours to spend, covering up, protecting with elaborate cages and boxes, with straw and brown paper and glass and polythene. Or perhaps they are simply uncannily lucky, or have magic powers. My winter garden is not like theirs. Most people's are not.

And yet, even without a flower or a green leaf showing, it can be a beautiful place, if you will only try to look on it with new eyes.

When you consider that you must live with it, in this state, for almost half of every year, you realise that such effort cannot be in vain. Bloom and blossom and fruit are come and gone, in a day, a week, a month at most, the grass withereth, the flower fadeth, and it is soon winter once more. So, on that January day, go outside, stand, look around at the garden. This is the time when you can see its shape, the bare bones of it, the lines and contours, the way the ground rises and falls, the whole design of it. The outline is not blurred or softened now by any foliage. In summer, the garden is a painting. In winter it is a piece of sculpture. If there are any hard and ugly lines, any blunt angles, now they are fully revealed, and perhaps you can see a way to soften them, round them off. If there are unsightly bits of fence or wall, gate or out-building, perhaps they can be disguised or obscured, or even done away with altogether.

You will see the delicate skeleton of any trees or shrubs, perhaps picked out by frost. Many a plain tree, which is passed over among the mass of others when in leaf, reveals all its elegance and grace when bare in winter.

I love the garden best on days of bright sun and brilliant blue sky and thick, thick frost, when the grass crunches underfoot and every twig has been iced over, the whole garden like a wedding cake.

But there *are* flowers to be had in winter, even in the very worst of the weather, and all the more to be enjoyed, standing out all the more bravely and clearly in their individual beauty, because they are so few and hard to find, come upon like rare jewels in the grass. The first snowdrops; and the winter aconites, worth planting by the hundred, under walls and trees, anywhere, to make a buttercup field in February. The common, ever-welcome winter-flowering jasmine; there is a great bush of it near to my own house, whose branches spring up and out in all directions, like a head of springy golden hair on a young girl, woven all in and out with starry flowers.

Dusty pink viburnum, like tiny powder-puffs, blooms on bare branches in early winter and smells ineffably sweet. Witch hazel, the healing plant, smells too, and will grow to a good height, and give golden flowers to gladden the cold heart. And when the year should be on the turn in March, and yet the winter lingers on, and the garden does not come to life, a little bush of magnolia stellata will give great joy, with its flowers of purest white. And all these are common enough and there are more. But I would rather not try desperately to make the garden bloom against its better self, month after winter month, forcing this, neurotically protecting that, ransacking the obscurest botanical manual in search of the other, and all in an effort to pretend that there is no such thing as winter. For a very few precious flowering things now are like single sweetmeats allowed only on Sundays in barren Lent.

In spring, the birds may nest in your garden, deep in the greenery; in summer, they will be about all day and on into the late evening, though you may not see or pay any heed to them, there is so much else in abundance, the birds are ten a penny. But in winter, if you will only feed them a few scraps, hang up a coconut or a net of nuts, break the ice on the pond or the trough to let them drink and clean, then the birds will creep close to you gratefully, hover about the window-ledges, hop on the terrace, the wall, the lawn, hunger making them bold. And then you can enjoy the fussy walk of the chaffinch, the companionability of the robin, the nervous never-stillness of the tits. These will be everyday English birds, sturdy, dependable, though on harsher days you may be favoured by rarer creatures – a fieldfare or a redwing, venturing into the shelter.

"I love the country in winter; one expects nothing and everything is a joy and a surprise. The first aconite! Does any flower in summer give the same pleasure? The blue-green blades of the daffodils and jonquils are firmly and strongly pushing through the cold brown earth; nothing in all the year gives such a sense of power and joy."

Mrs C. W. Earle

"When the leaves are down and the flower borders are bare one turns with a feeling of grateful admiration to the evergreen trees, plants and bushes. They are all the more to be appreciated because so many of them are now in their best and deepest coloured foliage. Holly, yew, bay and box are clothed in a kind of subdued splendour that is not only grateful to the eye but gladdening to the mind. Then all the greys and faint brown and silvery greens of treebole and branch, and the thin mist so frequent during the days of early winter, form just the right setting for the deep, rich colouring of the evergreens."

Gertrude Jekyll

Pleasures of the Autumn and Winter Garden

FINDING the last red apple, hanging by a thread from a bare branch.

Berries everywhere, blood-red against the evergreen.

A swag of mistletoe on the orchard bough.

Bonfires at dusk.

Fresh-sawn logs, neatly stacked against the wall.

The smell of frost at dawn.

Lifting the potatoes and slipping them into sacks.

The shed hung about with onion plaits.

Spiders' webs laced over fruit bushes.

The smell of horse manure, newly spread.

The first snowdrop, after the snow.

Viburnum blossom.

No weeding.

The Gardener

OF ALL human activities, apart from the procreation of children, gardening is the most optimistic and hopeful. The gardener is by definition one who plans for and believes and trusts in a future, whether in the short or the longer term. To sow seeds and plant out, to graft and propagate, whether it be peas and beans, apples and plums, roses and peonies, is to make one's own positive stake in that future, a gesture, declaring that there *will be* weeks, months, years ahead. And he who plants sapling trees, which will not arrive at their full maturity for fifty or a hundred years, is not only an optimist but a benefactor to coming generations.

Those who constantly think of war and dread its prospect, who see an end to mankind and his planet, whose spirits are shrivelled and hearts bowed down by the troubles and threats of the age, who refuse to have any hope, take any comfort, see the glimmer of any new dawn, should be gardeners. The gardener learns to be by turns daring and adventurous, tender and ruthless, meticulous and haphazard, gentle and patient. But above all, he learns to revel in today, while being ever hopeful of tomorrow.

Landscape Gardens

YOU DO not get the best inspiration for your own garden by sitting or walking alone in it, whether looking, thinking, dreaming, planning or criticising, nor even from perusing the very best books. It comes from going about, from looking at other people's gardens. From stopping the car in the middle of a strange village through which you chance to be passing, getting out and strolling, looking over walls and fences, parting loose bits of hedge to peer through; from finding a list of private gardens open to the public on summer Sundays, and visiting them to learn, as well as to enjoy, and to take tea. From looking down at front gardens from the top deck of a bus, or across at back gardens from the windows of a train. From being nosey. No gardener minds interest and attention from another.

And other people's gardens will provide plenty of lessons in what not to do with one's own, for there is a great deal of ugliness, brashness, messiness or over-neatness about, many gardens have things all out of proportion or out of keeping or ill-assorted, which saves anyone else from making the same mistakes.

But some gardens are inimitable, and are to be visited for that very fact; for their greatness and grandeur, impressiveness and scale, the inspiration of their design and skill of their creation. These are the great landscape gardens, the parks and messuages of important houses, designed by the celebrated men of gardening in past centuries, and maintained with love and devotion, with hard labour and a sense of duty, with much money. Knowing that you cannot compete, do not have to take note of translatable details, you can simply relax, breathe in the pure air, admire. Such gardens will not teach you what to do with your own, and so should not make you feel inferior, hopeless, dissatisfied. They are on a different, scarcely human, scale.

They are works of art, not merely places. You move about in them, immerse yourself, and for a short while become a part of them.

Long lawns, meticulously mown, stretch away, away, to a lake, upon which rare water-birds swim, and across which is placed a graceful bridge; a ha-ha will be there, beyond which you see the wilder part of the grounds, dotted with sheep; flights of stone steps lead up onto theatre lawns, or down towards gravelled terraces, in the centre of which, formally placed, are the ornamental pools, the fountains; you walk through pleached walks of hornbeams, laburnum alleys a hundred yards long, a succession of rose arches, towards grandiose herbaceous borders, high walls of rose-red brick against which fruit is espaliered. Beside the house will be the conservatories full of plumbago, peaches, camellias, lilies, smelling damp, earthy, aromatic. As you walk about the broad paths, you may come upon a grotto, a folly, a gazebo, and all manner of classical statues. There are numerous little summer-houses and rustic shelters, private bowers and arbours. The hedges are twenty foot high, carved here and there into peacocks.

Apart from its extensiveness, the glory of the great garden is its mass and variety of fine trees and shrubs. Nowhere else do they spread so, assume such magnificent proportions, have such massive presence. There may be some chinoiserie, a wooden pagoda, or other oriental conceit; doric columns; a primrose dell; a leafy glade through which narrow, winding paths descend. In spring, rhododen-drons astonish, in autumn, every colour of deciduous leaf. In winter, the whole design and structure will be made visible, and all the sky revealed, as light pours in unexpectedly. Blenheim and Stowe, Stourhead and Rousham, Woburn and Chatsworth, are as wonderful on the clear, bright days of winter as in the height of June.

Such places, such gardeners, will never come again but, because they are few, and precious survivors, they are even more to be cherished. This is gardening of more spacious, elaborate, uncluttered ages, a different art. It does not translate to our own, or adjust to a more modest and private scale. But the spirit of those great gardens can bring harmony, order, tranquillity and breadth to the soul.

The Maze Garden

'HARRIS asked me if I'd ever been in the maze at Hampton Court. He said he went in once to show somebody else the way. He had studied it on a map, and it was so simple that it seemed foolish – hardly worth the twopence charged for admission. He said "We'll just go in here, so that you can say you've been, but it's very simple. It's absurd to call it a maze. You keep on taking the first turning to the right. We'll just walk round for ten minutes and then go and get some lunch."

They met some people soon after they had got inside, who said they'd been there for three quarters of an hour, and had had about enough of it. Harris told them they could follow him if they liked; he was just going in, and then would turn round and go out again. They said it was very kind of him, and fell behind, and followed.

They picked up various other people who wanted to get it over as they went along, until they absorbed all the persons in the maze. People who had given up all hopes of ever getting in or out, or of ever seeing their home and friends again, plucked up their courage at

the sight of Harris, and his party, and joined
the procession, blessing him ... Harris kept
on turning to the right, but it seemed a long
way, and his cousin said he supposed it was a
very big maze.

"Oh, one of the largest in Europe," said
Harris.

"Yes, it must be," replied the cousin,
"because we've walked a good two miles
already." '

Jerome K. Jerome

The Water Garden

WATER transforms a garden. No other single element brings such life and light, such movement and interest, such refreshment and balm, not even the rushing and whispering of a million leaves on the breeze of a summer night.

Most blessed of all gardeners are those who have a natural source of water in their grounds, around which everything grows; a stream trickling through long grass or shallow ditch or over pebbles, or a woodland pool in a glade. Over many years, all manner of plants that love damp places will have established themselves, so that it has only to be kept clear of entangling weeds and any over-vigorous and spreading growth, and otherwise left quite to itself, to be enjoyed, a precious inheritance. But bringing water into a garden which has none is a relatively simple task, and will give great reward for little trouble. A shallow pond can be constructed in a day, left to settle, and then planted with lilies, irises and water-loving grasses which will soon take root and make themselves at home. A small fountain can be added for surprisingly little cost, and will splash up and over upon itself most soothingly. If the garden slopes, or a corner of it can be made to do so, and then a rockery constructed, a waterfall can be established which will flow down into the pond or stream and away. A raised pond can be built of stone, or even bought ready-made with a wide, flat ledge to sit upon.

Nothing that I have ever added to my own garden has given me more pleasure than the little pond. Sitting beside it, listening to the soft plop of water upon water, soothes and stills; watching the play of sunlight and shadow on the surface, peering down into the darkness of it in search of the hidden fish, being surprised by the arrival of a dragonfly, the opening of a pure white lily one early morning – all add delight to the day.

"Water is the most interesting object in a landscape, and the happiest circumstance in a retired recess; captivates the eye at a distance,

invites approach, and is delightful when near; it refreshes an open exposure; it animates a shade; cheers the dreariness of a waste, and enriches the most crowded view; in form, in style, and in extent, may be made equal to the greatest compositions, or adapted to the least; it may spread in a calm expanse to sooth the tranquillity of a peaceful scene; or hurrying along a devious course add splendour to a gay, and extravagance to a romantic, situation."

Thomas Whateley

"I have pockets of cement made at irregular intervals at the edges of the fountain to hold water-plants and such things, which then appear reflected on the surface of the water, not as they grow against a dark shrub or a group of Italian canes or bamboos, but against the blue sky above them – an endless pleasure to those who notice such things. A piece of water, however small, and the sound of water falling from a small fountain, or even from the raised tap, if the tank is near a wall, is such an added enjoyment to life on a hot summer's day, not to mention the infinite superiority for watering of having water that has been exposed to the sun and air."

Mrs C. W. Earle

My Fantasy Garden

EVERY garden has its own particular feature, something unique, which is its focus and its strength, and which gives it its character and distinguishes it from every other garden. It may be its situation or shape or a certain aspect or vista within it, or else something individual – a tree or shrub, unusual or fine, an archway, a gate, an old wall, a summer-house, a perfect lawn. You have only to discover and recognise that individuality, and allow it to express itself, or at least, do nothing to destroy or detract from it. Like the charm of a person, it may not be revealed to you at once, or even for a year or more, but if you live in humble and expectant mood with a garden, in the course of time you will come to know it. And if you begin with a bare and muddy acre, unplanted, unshaped, then you can help to mould the character of the garden yourself.

Once I left the gardens of my childhood, the first of my adult life was not purely my own at all, but shared between a cluster of houses; though I had one small flowerbed outside my front window, which I always filled with stocks and petunias, and some flagstones on which I set roses in tubs, outside the back.

The rest was a pleasant enough, but uninteresting, raised lawn, but though the houses themselves were new they had been built upon the site of a single, old one, which had had a garden full of mature trees. Several of these had been left, and among them all, the best, which I could see from every window of my house, was a small, gnarled and bent crab apple, up against the old brick wall. In spring it flowered, in autumn it fruited, and all winter through its bare branches made a strange, yet delightful shape to be admired against the sky. It lent a distinctiveness, and, more, a personality, a spirit, to that plain green space.

Our first married garden was long and narrow, and its delights were a wall which surrounded it completely, and up which grew a riot of untamed honeysuckle, that scented all our summer nights, with, nearby, a very tall white lilac. The lilac was a mixed blessing. It shut out some of the light from an already dark house, flowered only every other year, and left an ugly mass of rusty brown dead blooms behind it for several weeks. Yet when it was in its full glory, foaming white, for that part of the month of May it was quite forgiven.

And then we came to the country, to a garden whose spirit is in its little magic apple

tree, which stands sturdily against a low stone
wall, beyond which the land stretches away
and away, for miles, down meadows to a
stream fringed with willow trees, and divided
into lots of squares and rectangles by yards of
old hawthorn and blackthorn hedge. From
this garden, at every season, we look out, and
the sky, in every weather, seems to be part of
what we grow. Here, apart from our apple
tree, anything tall is out of keeping, besides
being impractical when the wind blows. It is a
low, almost flat garden, and needs to be kept
so, for nothing ought to detract from the
great landscape that lies below.

Yet when we arrived here, we found a host
of incongruous things, planted by someone
with no eye and no foresight or imagination;
a huge holly bush and a Christmas tree which
had firmly taken root and flourished were
stuck in the middle of the view, and a japonica
had been left to spread wildly in all directions,
like an unkempt head of hair, and there was
that scourge of all gardens, a weeping willow,
already reached to fifteen feet or so, and set to
tower to thirty or forty, obscuring the sight of
a particularly beautiful, up-sloping hill. The

borders were full of Queen Elizabeth roses, those vigorous, long-legged ladies, seven feet tall.

We have spent six years getting rid of what was out of keeping, out of proportion, ugly, or plain dull, always trying to clear the way for the view beyond. But we have planted too. I have put in a great many things I have either long loved, or recently discovered, and been ruthless with what I do not care for, because, as I grow older, I understand that I do not have to have a single thing in my garden that does not please me. There is a lot of fencing, and we have trained clematis and honeysuckle up and over it wherever we can, and old stone walls for those two most perfect of climbing roses, New Dawn and Madame Alfred Carrière.

I loathe flowers coloured orange or red or, apart from sunflowers and daffodils, yellow, and so I simply do not have any, but pink, instead, and a great deal of white, and some blue, beds of delphiniums, lupins and phlox, many peonies, English roses and old, shrub roses, white papaver, a magnolia stellata, and dozens of old, laced pinks, clove-scented, edging the paths.

There is a small pond, though the fish do not last for long there, because the heron is a regular scavenger at dawn, but it has a fountain, whose sound delights and soothes me.

For the bleak days of February and March, I planted hundreds of bulbs, a tedious chore, but one for which I am every year rewarded, with anemone blanda, iris reticulata, snowdrops, speciosum crocuses, very small and delicate daffodils.

To satisfy my desire for a real orchard in which to wander, I planted a dozen dwarf apple trees, which have taken well and give us some delicious fruit in unusual varieties. And yet I think that they were a mistake, and do not sort well with the garden, and when they die or blow down, they will not be replaced, and my orchard must be in some other place, some other life.

Otherwise, there is grass for the children to play on, and a good, plain rectangle of kitchen garden close to the house, and yet from which I can still look up and see for all those miles, there is a herb patch and a terrace for whatever takes my fancy, to grow tomatoes or lilies, geraniums or chives in big pots, change and change about.

ALWAYS, like a child who is never content, I want things I cannot have: a waterfall, a stream running through a leafy glade, bluebell woodland, a rose arch and a pleached walk, an arbour with a gazebo, lily ponds, a ha-ha, a wide-spreading copper beech with a swing hanging from a low branch in the middle of an emerald lawn, a lake, camellias, plumbago and peach trees in a long conservatory, a fig, a maze, little box hedges, a knot garden, an orchard full of bee hives and sheep.

In my mind, the ideal, the fantasy garden lies, forever unreachable and unattainable, beyond the door through which I still cannot pass, except in dreams, except in dreams.

But here and now, it is early spring with sunshine and a fresh breeze blowing, and a robin sits on the watering can. There is work to be done.